DUNLOP

Courtesy Norman Hyde

John
HANCOX 82

TRIUMPH
TRIDENT

Ivor Davies

CONTENTS

Foulis

Haynes

ISBN 0 85429 352 3

A FOULIS Motorcycling Book

First published 1984

© **Haynes Publishing Group**

Published by:
Haynes Publishing Group
Sparkford, Yeovil,
Somerset BA22 7JJ

Distributed in USA by:
Haynes Publications Inc.
861 Lawrence Drive, Newbury Park,
California 91320, USA

Cover design: Rowland Smith
Page Layout: Mike King
Photographs: Andrew Morland
and Ivor Davies
Road tests: Motorcycle Mechanics
and Motor Cycle News courtesy of
EMAP National Publications Ltd.
Printed in England by: J.H. Haynes &
Co. Ltd

Titles in the *Super Profile* series

Further titles in this series will be published at regular
intervals. For information on new titles please contact your
bookseller or write to the publisher.

FOREWORD

If the Triumph Thunderbird was 'the first of the Superbikes', then the Triumph Trident can fairly lay claim to being the last – at least of the British variety. But whereas the Thunderbird was rolling off the production lines at Meriden for seventeen years, the Trident lasted a mere six, killed off along with the British manufacturing industry in 1975. However, in its brief span of life it made a tremendous impact as its glorious exhaust note boomed victoriously across the Isle of Man and other circuits in Europe and USA. Who will ever forget the starts of those early Anglo-American Match Races when both teams were mounted on Tridents (or the BSA equivalent, the Rocket 3) – was there ever such a crescendo of sound to stun the ears of the enthusiasts!

The Trident came on the scene too late to save the British industry, or what was left of it. Fatal inactivity in the face of ever increasing competition from Japan delayed its introduction by several years and when it did arrive, the very sophisticated 750cc CB750 Honda was announced at almost the same time. This was the model which really set the motorcycle world off on a completely new tack in much the same way as Edward Turner's Speed Twin had done in 1938.

The Trident story is a tangled one set against a background of financial problems, industrial relations chaos, Government interference and finally the demise of a world famous and much respected British industry. Whilst it is impossible to avoid reference to some of these background factors, my story, as far as possible, is about the motorcycle itself and I am grateful for this opportunity to tell it, as the Trident was a superb British motorcycle, the last of its kind, and it is a story which should be told.

My employment as Publicity Manager at Triumph terminated, after 30 years or so, at about the same time as the industry folded, so I know something about Trident history first hand, but that knowledge has been widened enormously by the helpful co-operation of Doug Hele, one of the two architects of Trident design and success (Bert Hopwood was the other), who provided a wealth of information on the early days of the three cylinder concept and its development. He was also kind enough to read through the text when it was finished.

I am also indebted to Les Williams and Norman Hyde, two stalwarts of the Trident team at Meriden, both of whom have, independently created miniature Trident industries of their own, building Trident derivatives of shattering performance, supplying parts and generally keeping the Trident flag flying. Their willingness to dip deep into their memories for facts and figures and their co-operation with some of the photography was invaluable.

Andrew Morland took most of the photographs and these have been augmented by some from my files. Two long standing members of the Triumph Owners MCC have provided 'Owners' Views' and their opinions on anything relating to Triumph are always worth having. As in any family, the Club can be merciless in its criticism of the marque within its ranks, but its loyalty is unswerving and woe betide anyone from outside who is uncomplimentary! Roy Bacon's book *Triumph Twins & Triples* was, as always, a mine of information for confirmation of dates and data.

Like all things mechanical, the Trident had its faults but they were not many and were completely overshadowed by its qualities as a 'rider's motorcycle' – it was fast, it steered to a hair, it could notch up big mileages with minimum attention and was easy to work on when necessary.

It was a credit to its designers, developers and the Triumph and BSA factories where it was made. Also, in racing guise, it was almost unbeatable in those heady days of the early seventies.

Ivor Davies

HISTORY

It was ironic that the last motorcycle produced at the great BSA works at Small Heath Birmingham, was a Triumph! The NVT (Norton Villiers Triumph) Group, a Government-inspired organisation which merged BSA/Triumph and Norton Villiers in 1973 in an effort to save the industry, had made a decision to move Triumph production to Small Heath and close the Triumph works at Meriden, near Coventry. The subsequent blockade of Meriden by the workers is a story which is too well known to bear repeating here, but it did result in Bonneville production remaining at Meriden and the Trident moving to Small Heath. This operation was not without its problems as the Triumph workers refused to allow the Triumph tooling or drawings to be released, with the result that Small Heath had to produce duplicate tools, which they did with great skill, but of course at considerable cost. In the meantime, a lot of work had been done to update the specification of the Meriden Trident so that by the time the Small Heath track started to roll, a virtually new model, the T160, made its appearance. As a Triumph man I well recall my disbelief at seeing the railings around the BSA works bearing striking coloured posters

announcing the production there of the new Triumph Trident! It must have seemed even more incredible to the workers at Small Heath.

Now the Trident has gone, and BSA has gone. It seems impossible that the great factory with its colossal output of armaments during both world wars should be no more. Without BSA it is quite likely that hostilities would have gone on much longer than they did. However, this is really the end of the Trident story, so let us get back to the beginning to tell how this remarkable motorcycle came into being.

The Trident was unusual in that it had three cylinders, a configuration that had not been seen before on a motorcycle designed for relatively high production figures. MV produced a very successful three cylinder racer for Agostini and Laverda have had threes in production in recent years; there have also been several three cylinder two-strokes, but generally speaking, both in the two and four wheel world, the three cylinder engine has been neglected until recently. However it is rumoured that one of B.L.'s experimental 'economy cars' has a three cylinder engine. Also, going way back, the 15 hp Rolls Royce car of 1905 had a three cylinder engine with overhead inlet and side exhaust valves, an arrangement retained by RR on its engines until comparatively recently. Yet the three has many positive advantages and it is strange that it has not been exploited more vigorously. With its 120 degree crankshaft it can be made to run very smoothly, vastly better than the conventional vertical twin. Also, and this is particularly beneficial on a motorcycle, it is narrower than a four and can be placed across the frame without protruding to any great extent on each side like the many fours in the market today (not to mention a certain very celebrated flat twin!).

In the case of the Trident it was expediency as much as

anything else which dictated the number of cylinders. Anyone familiar with the Triumph twin cylinder engine will see that the Trident design is basically the same. By designing it this way, it could obviously be produced more quickly because the techniques and tooling would be very similar to those used on the twin. The object was to get a superbike class motorcycle into production rapidly, to cope with the competition, to produce some income, and most importantly, give the company some time to look ahead and design the models of the future. None of these things, in fact, happened as planned, but the story is a very interesting one and it mainly concerns Bert Hopwood, director and general manager at Meriden, and his chief development engineer, Doug Hele. As a designer and engineer, Hopwood spent a working lifetime in the industry and many famous motorcycles originated on his drawing board, the BSA Golden Flash and the Norton Dominator to name but two. Hele is probably our greatest development engineer and he and Hopwood formed a unique team firstly at BSA, then Norton, and finally at Triumph. Here they came to the conclusion that any engine above 650cc would have to have more cylinders than two because of the inherent vibration problems which beset the 650, due in part to the considerable increase in power which had been extracted from it since its introduction in 1950. The idea of the 500 twin with an extra cylinder 'tacked on' to make it a 750 seemed attractive and design work started in 1964, the first engine running on the test bed in January 1965. This first engine retained the same 63 x 80 mm bore and stroke dimensions as the original 500cc Speed Twin; the cylinder barrel was also cast iron and the primary drive was by three gears. This first engine soon produced 59 bhp at 8000 rpm which was a good start. Following this, extensive road mileage proved that the three was a much smoother engine than the twin and that the increase in weight was nothing to worry about. Looking to the future, the company at this point was working on a new approach to its range where by utilising a standard bore/stroke dimension of 67 x 70 mm, a 250 single, a 500 twin and a 750 three could be produced. The 250 single went to BSA and the 500 twin did not materialise due to the fact that the regulations for the Daytona 200 for 1966 insisted that a factory must have produced 200 units before a bike could be raced. It was not feasible to redesign the 500 *and* produce 200 units in the time, so the 500 remained at 69 x 65.5 mm, but a new 750 three was started with the 67 x 70 mm dimension. At the same time, many changes were made following on the experience gained with the original engine. Head temperatures were reduced by raising the rocker box floor above the head joint and an aluminium barrel stopped cylinder head distortion at the joint with the barrel. Big ends and main bearings were modified by the use of special materials supplied by Vandervell. Nitrited camshafts cured the problem of cam wear, and so on. All the development findings were incorporated into the specification of the production models, which were finally announced to the public in March 1968, but potential UK purchasers had to wait until the following year, all initial supplies both of the Trident and the BSA Rocket 3 going to the United States.

It is not possible to tell the story of the Trident without some reference to its close relation, the BSA Rocket 3. Both models were designed at the same time to provide both marques with a competitive superbike. All engines, for both the Trident and the Rocket 3, were manufactured at the BSA works in Birmingham and were virtually identical except that the cylinders on the Rocket 3 engines were inclined slightly forward and

timing cover shapes were different. The running gear and chassis of the two models were also different, BSA using their usual twin down tube frame and Triumph sticking to their traditional single front down tube. Both frames posed a problem as to the disposal of the centre cylinder exhaust pipe, which branched into two on leaving the port to join immediately with its neighbour on either side, thus reducing the number of pipes to two, which ran along both sides of the machine to the silencers in the normal way. Seats and other equipment on both models followed the normal practices of the marque so that the Group could not really be accused of 'badge engineering' as had happened at AMC and elsewhere.

At this time, Triumph were racing, very successfully, the 500cc Daytona-type twins and the 650 Bonneville, in production events. Development of the three as a racer had not been considered as, at the time, the 500s were still lapping as fast as bigger capacity machines. However, in 1969 Percy Tait raced a factory-entered three in that year's Hutchinson Hundred and finished sixth. The object of the exercise was to see how the three handled rather than to win the race, the engine being a standard unit. The result was encouraging and in the autumn of 1969, some work was done on an engine to improve its performance by fitting certain proven components similar to those used on the successful 500 racer. This resulted in an output of 78 bhp but showed up unreliability in areas like the ignition system. At this time interest was growing in Formula 750 or Daytona type racing, where basically standard specifications were required, but quite extensive modifications were permitted. The value of this to a manufacturer was obvious. He could test new solutions to problems and build up a store of knowledge which could later find its way into production. Production racing, on the other hand, banned all development of

this kind. Another factor which entered the scene at this time was a change in the rules by the Americans who had hitherto limited ohv engines to 500cc and side valves to 750cc. Now races would be open to all 750 types and this led to a decision at Triumph to enter the 'threes' at Daytona in 1970. The 500s had been very successful in this race, winning in both 1966 and 1967, but the effort planned for the 'threes' was on a much more ambitious scale. Six bikes would go and a lot of new design work was required before they would be raceworthy. A five-speed gearbox by Rod Quaife and a completely new frame by Rob North were two major items. Fairings based on wind tunnel research made a big contribution to a one-way speed of 164 mph (157 mph mean) on test.

At Daytona the machines caused a great sensation by recording the three fastest times in the qualifying tests, Gene Romero averaging 157.34 mph with 165.44 mph through a speed trap on the front straight. In the race overheating caused problems due to the fairings directing hot air on to the carburettors, but Romero and Castro finished second and third behind Dick Mann on a Honda 4 after Nixon had led for much of the race as he did again in 1971. Back home these problems were soon ironed out and attention was turned to Production racing. In the Production TT in the Isle of Man, Malcolm Uphill won by 1.6 seconds from Peter Williams on his works Norton Commando and in the Bol d'Or 24 hour race in France, against strong works opposition from all the leading Japanese and European factories, Paul Smart and Tom Dickie brought their Trident home first, at an average speed of 76.51 mph for a distance of 1828 miles (24 laps better than the previous record).

Then followed two years of almost unbroken success for these phenomenal three cylinder roadster-based racers. Virtually every major Production and Formula 750 race was won in Europe and USA. A list of some of these events will be found later in the book. Race records and lap records went by the board but perhaps the most incredible victories were those scored by John Cooper who beat Giacomo Agostini, the reigning World Champion, not once, but twice. At that time, Agostini's 500cc three cylinder MV was the most advanced grand prix racer the world had seen, which made Cooper's victories even more remarkable. That a simple unsophisticated roadster-based racer could do this, is some measure of the skill and dedication put into the development of these machines by Doug Hele and his team, not to mention the supreme ability of Cooper as a rider. In addition to this, and probably equally remarkable, was the record of one single machine nicknamed 'Slippery Sam' which won the Isle of Man Production TT for five consecutive years 1971 to 1975. Such a feat deserves separate story and this follows later.

(It should perhaps be mentioned here that the name on Cooper's bike actually read BSA, but the machines were identical and labels were frequently changed depending on commercial requirements.)

Such was our confidence in these superb machines that in 1972 I gambled on winning both the Production TT and F750 races in the Isle of Man and hired a film crew to 'shoot' both events. As it happened we did just that and the resulting film *Island Double* was a notable addition to our film library. If we had not won, I would not have been popular with the management when they received the bill!

So what was the effect of these racing successes on the model that the man-in-the-street could buy? Obviously some of the development rubbed off; in fact we find that a major face-lift took place at this time which Bert Hopwood

described as 'a rejuvenation of our triple cylinder motorcycle featuring much of our world beating racing model'. Race breeding with a vengeance! This was scheduled for production early in 1973. The engine unit had been uprated from 750 to 830cc and a power output of 67 bhp at 8300 rpm achieved. Electric starting was incorporated and some crafty work on the exhaust system not only improved the mid-range torque but reduced the exhaust noise by 4 db. The intention was that this model would replace both the Trident and the Rocket 3. However, for various reasons to do with the difficult financial situation in which the Group found itself at the time, the model did not progress beyond the prototype stage, although we shall see later that the work was not wasted. Incidentally, the name suggested for this machine was 'Thunderbird III' – a nice touch!

Heavy losses in 1972/73 led to a crisis situation and Government intervention which resulted in a merger between BSA/Triumph and Norton/Villiers as has been described at the beginning of this story. The Trident which eventually emerged down the Small Heath tracks owed a lot to the Thunderbird III prototype produced some time before. Known as the T160 it boasted electric starting, a 5 speed gearbox and disc brakes front and rear. The engine, still a 750, was the BSA sloping cylinder version which reduced the congestion at the rear of the block. This was a very handsome motorcycle and would undoubtedly have sold in considerable numbers if the Group had survived.

The first Trident was built on 23rd August 1968 and the last one on 28th April 1976. In between 27,480 were produced plus 5,897 Rocket 3s. Its life span exactly covered the stormy period of industrial relations and financial problems which beset the Group. It was designed at Meriden and was made there until the transfer to

Birmingham in 1974. It survived all the problems of the period and was intended to be the first of the range of models scheduled to be designed and built at the Small Heath factory. However, in the face of the over-powering foreign competition and all the trauma which the company had been through, there was no way that it could continue. So the famous names of Triumph, BSA and Norton, as we knew them, came to an end and it was a sad day for an industry which had led the world since before the Great War. But the Trident had made its mark. No other single machine (and I mean single machine!) in history had won five TTs in a row and its glorious howling exhaust note will be remembered by enthusiasts the world over long after the demented scream of the two-strokes will have been forgotten.

5 in a row for 'Slippery Sam'!

The possibility of the same motorcycle winning five TTs in five consecutive years would have been the subject of derisive laughter in Isle of Man racing circles – until it actually happened – and the motorcycle concerned was a Triumph Trident nicknamed 'Slippery Sam' for reasons which will be explained shortly.

Slippery Sam started life in 1970 as one of three similar models prepared at Meriden for that year's Production TT. One of these three ridden by Malcolm Uphill won the race. Malcolm will be remembered as the rider who, the year before, won this race on a Bonneville at 99.99 mph, twice breaking the 100 mph for a lap, the first time this figure had been recorded by a production motorcycle. In the 1970 event, Sam was ridden by Tom Dickie, a last minute substitute. Being of small stature and unfamiliar with Sam's ways, he fumbled the Le

Mans start and was actually last away. Probably annoyed by this, he rode to such good purpose thereafter that he overtook almost the entire field to finish a splendid fourth. Later in the same year Sam gained his nickname at the Bol d'Or 24 hour race in France, where some malfunction in the lubrication system caused oil to be spewed out until the bike and riders (Percy Tait and Steve Jolly) were covered – nevertheless they managed to finish fifth despite additional pit stops to replenish the oil supply. In 1971, Sam, with no oil anywhere other than in the right places, won the Production TT in the hands of Ray Pickrell at 100.07 mph, the first time this race had been won at a three figure average. 1972 saw the factory faced with financial problems and production racing was chopped off the schedule. This put Sam into retirement, in fact the machine was relegated to the factory cellar in a part dismantled state. Some time later, as the 1972 June races got nearer, Ray Pickrell asked if he could borrow Sam, so Les Williams, race shop manager, took Sam home and set about preparing it in his own workshop.

Permission was a last minute affair and by that time Les was on holiday in the Isle of Man, so Sam was ridden to the Island by another member of the Meriden race shop, Fred Swift. Once again Ray finished first, with a new lap record of 101.61 mph. Following this, Les bought Sam from the factory and thereafter was solely responsible for its tuning and maintenance.

In 1973, Tony Jefferies asked to borrow Sam and after a strong challenge by Peter Williams (Norton), whose gearbox finally gave up the ghost, Sam (and Tony) notched up the third consecutive win. Mick Grant was the rider in 1974 and once again the opposition was swept aside to give Sam his fourth win. Surely it could not happen again – but it did! As if to make things more difficult for Sam, the ACU increased the length of the race to 10 laps and called for two riders per machine. There was an amusing twist to Sam's last victory. NVT had entered Norton Commandos and they asked Les Williams if they could borrow Sam so that NVT would be represented by both marques in the Group. Dave Croxford and Alex George were the two riders and they won, with a new lap record by Alex George at 102.82 mph. That was Sam's 5th and final win.

Now Sam has retired on loan to the National Motorcycle Museum, which is expecting to open its doors to the public in 1984, and enthusiasts will be able to look at Sam and marvel at his record. It should not be forgotten either than in addition to the Isle of Man wins, Sam scored many other successes in between, both on UK and Continental circuits. Truly a unique motorcycle!

Production TT Isle of Man (1 lap = $37\frac{3}{4}$ miles)

Year	Race Length	Riders	Entrant	Position	Speed mph
1970	5 laps	Tom Dickie	Eddie Dow	4th	94.14
1971	4 laps	Ray Pickrell	Triumph Eng. Co.	1st	100.07
1972	4 laps	Ray Pickrell	Boyers of Bromley	1st	100.00
1973	4 laps	Tony Jefferies	Allan Jefferies	1st	95.62
1974	4 laps	Mick Grant	A. Bennett Ltd	1st	99.72
1975	10 laps	D.Croxford/ A. George	NVT	1st	99.60

'Slippery Sam' Specification

Engine	Bore/stroke 67 x 70 mm overbored +010in – capacity 749cc Carburetters (3) Amal Concentric 626 (27mm) Main jet 200 Throttle valve $3\frac{1}{2}$. Compression ratio 11.5:1 Hepolite pistons. S & W Valve springs. Triumph TH6 camshafts. Ignition by Lucas battery and coil 6V. Bendix contact breakers. Fixed advance 38° BTDC. Champion N34R or N81R plugs. bhp (est) 72/75. Max rpm 8500.
Transmission	5 speed Quaife CR gear cluster. Standard clutch with HD spring. Renold racing chains. Oils – Engine Castrol R30, Gearbox Castrol R40.
Frame	Lightened standard frame with lifted bottom rails to increase ground clearance.
Suspension	Front Triumph telescopic. Rear Girling dampers 100/168
Wheels	Borrani rims WM3x19. TYRES Dunlop 4.10 x 19 TT100 or Dunlop NR83 rear, NR76 front.
Brakes front	Pre 1974 – Fontana 250mm 4 leading shoe drum brake. Ferodo linings. 1974 on – Triumph hydraulic, twin discs. Lockheed calipers and master cylinder.
Brakes rear	Triumph 7 in drum QD. Ferodo linings.
Fuel tank	by Don Woodward
Seat	by PP Seating
Fairing	by Screen & Plastic
Weight	with full oil tank – 402 lbs.

EVOLUTION

I have already described how the Trident came into being through the combined work of Bert Hopwood and Doug Hele at Meriden in the early sixties, but it was a long time reaching the market place for various reasons. Hopwood says it should and could have been in production much earlier, if only management had made some positive decisions about it. As it was, it was not until 1968 that it finally arrived. Many precious years had been lost during which time the Japanese fortified their hold on the market until they were unassailable. To those familiar with the layout of the Triumph twin, the three cylinder Trident T150 will be seen as a natural progression. In effect it is the 500 twin with an extra cylinder added. Like the twin it has gear driven camshafts fore and aft of the block, with pushrods in tubes between the cylinders. 67 x 70 mm bore and stroke give a capacity of 740cc. The heart of the engine is the three throw crankshaft. Made in the BSA forge, the forging was reheated and twisted to provide the 120 degree throws. When the forge closed in 1970, an outside supplier used more conventional methods. The two inner main bearings are plain, but ball and roller bearings are used for the drive and timing sides respectively. The rocker gears again

follow twin cylinder practice, with separate boxes for inlet and exhaust rockers, bolted to the alloy head.

The engine is set across the frame in the normal way, with the primary drive to the four-speed gearbox on the left-hand side. One departure from twin cylinder practice is that the alternator is mounted on the timing cover instead of the primary chaincase. This was done to avoid excessive overhang. The cylinder block is die-cast alloy, the rods are light alloy, big-ends are plain and the 9:1 pistons carry one scraper and two compression rings.

Three separate 27mm Amal Concentric carburetters supply the mixture, controlled by a positive linkage to the twistgrip, a single spring supplying the return action. Three sets of contact points are driven from the exhaust camshaft, and three separate coils are located together beneath the seat. Conventional dry sump lubrication is employed, with a separate six pint oil tank feeding a gear type pump, the supply returning to the tank via an oil cooler mounted below the leading edge of the fuel tank. The gearbox casing is an extension of the centre crankcase section and the four-speed gearbox follows normal Triumph practice except for the clutch, which is a Borg & Beck diaphragm single plate unit on car lines. Kickstarter and footchange pedals are located on the right-hand side.

This whole unit fitted neatly into a Bonneville-type frame, with a single front down tube and a braced single top tube. Down below, twin engine rails joined the front and saddle down tubes and a bolted-on sub frame completed the job. The front forks are standard Triumph as on the twins, complete with gaiters and headlamp bracket. The 19 inch front wheel incorporated an 8 inch 2LS brake and was shod with a Dunlop 3.25 in. section K70 tyre. The rear tyre is a 4.10 in. Dunlop K81 fitted to a 19 inch WM3 rim. Rear suspension is

conventional, with Girling units, and the rear brake a stock 7 inch drum as used on other models in the range. The tank, side panels and mudguards are catalogued as 'aquamarine' and the frame, forks, etc black as usual. Behind the large plated headlamp, a 'binnacle' houses the speedometer, tachometer, ammeter and warning lights for oil pressure and main beam. A steering damper is fitted.

Outside stylists had been brought in to work on the Trident. Why this was done is a mystery because if there was one thing they could do well at Meriden it was to make the motorcycles look good and the blending shapes, initially the work of Edward Turner, were an established and recognisable feature worldwide. However, the management of the day decided that something new was needed (what is known today as a 'new image') and the result was a slab sided tank, totally foreign to Triumph, and silencers with three little exit pipes. There were other things too and the result was not unpleasing, but it was *not* a Triumph and the market said so. It was a good motorcycle, it went well, but customers were a little wary at first. Three cylinders were unusual and the motorcycling fraternity has never really liked anything that did not conform fairly closely to the accepted norm of the day. One of the clever things about the original 1938 Speed Twin was the fact that it looked like a two port single of which there were plenty about at the time. However, a few road tests soon convinced the faithful that the Trident (or T150 was a real flyer and even if it did not look too much like a Triumph, it probably *was* one and would be alright. On this subject I would like to quote a few lines here from that admirable American book *The Motorcycle World* by Phil Schilling

'Norton and Triumph wanted "new" written all over their 750s. They resorted to stylised newness. The Norton Commando flaunted a fibreglass tail section on its seat, and the Triumph Trident carried ray-gun mufflers and a creased and kneaded breadloaf gas tank ... Triumph's American clientele would not accept the Flash Gordon getup on the new three cylinder. Americans refused to buy the Hallowe'en-look Triumph. In the Triumph customers' eyes the new 750 triple had to look like a Triumph; the present had to fit in with the past. If the motorcycle had been entirely fresh, the Trident might have uncovered a new following with no ties to tradition. That never happened. Fundamentally, the Trident was a conservative machine which appealed to conservative motorcyclists. Very quickly the Trident assumed the classic Triumph look'.

From this revealing piece it would seem that the poor British manufacturer could never win. When he brought out the same old bikes year after year he was accused of being a stick-in-the-mud. When he did finally bring out something different, no one would buy it until he had made it look like the old ones again! So for America, Triumph's most important market, the Trident rapidly assumed a genuine Triumph appearance once more, but retained its 'Flash Gordon getup' for most other markets.

So much for the 1969, or first, Trident. For the 1970 season the machine remained unchanged, apart from a few minor items which were tidied up in the light of experience. The colour scheme also carried on into the new season. For 1971, the whole BSA/Triumph range was re-vamped and vast sums of money were spent very wastefully in announcing this to the world through a big function in the West End of London. The re-vamping comprised mainly a new frame which put the seat so high that unless you were 6 foot 3 inches or taller, you could not reach the ground when sitting astride. I recall the occasion when all senior

sales personnel were invited to Umberslade Hall, the BSA Group Research Centre, to view the new models. Most of us were practising motorcyclists and our first reaction was to complain about the seat height (I am only 5ft 6½ ins!). A lot of the Umberslade staff were not practising motorcyclists and our complaint was laughed off. The company was to pay for it dearly later on when sales resistance world-wide forced expensive modifications to be made. Although this disastrous frame did not feature on the Trident, a number of the other changes did. The new 'slimline' fork legs were of polished aluminium and there were no gaiters. The headlamp brackets were now fashioned out of thin plated wire-like rod, presumably to save cost and weight. New brakes front and rear had conical hubs. The front mudguard lost several inches from its lower end, presumably in the interests of sporting appearance.

Megaphone type silencers replaced the original design with its three tail pipes (oddly enough this three pipe design was always to be seen on the works racers where it gave excellent results). Front and rear flashing indicators were fitted, plus a few other changes, mostly cosmetic. The engine and gearbox remained unchanged. Tank finish became what was described in the catalogue as 'Spring Gold or Black'.

In 1972, the colour scheme changed again to regal purple and the gearing was lowered fractionally to improve flexibility. Late in the season a five-speed gearbox appeared and the type number changed to T150V. Also a new model, the X75 Hurricane, was announced, intended primarily for sale in the United States. It was styled by American Craig Vetter. This was a model years ahead of its time, at least as far as appearance was concerned. In a concession to the 'chopper' craze, it had lengthened fork stanchions which increased the wheelbase to 60 inches. A one-piece glassfibre

fairing enclosed the tank and swept down both sides to just above the gearbox. The 'fenders' were reduced to minimal proportions. Many new Japanese models look very similar in their general outline today, but the Vetter was years ahead. The BSA sloping engine was used in a Trident frame and three megaphone type silencers were piled one on top of the other on the offside of the rear wheel. It did not achieve any great success at the time and only about a thousand or so were made. A good example today, if it could be found, would probably command a high price.

By this time, Tridents destined for the USA had reverted to the traditional Triumph bulbous tank, but the slab-sided one was retained for some markets. 1973 saw some major changes, not in the power unit area but once again in the fringe items. Gaiters were back on the forks and substantial headlamp brackets re-appeared in place of the 'plated wire' ones. A full length front mudguard came back and, most important of all, a 10 inch hydraulically-operated disc brake replaced the drum on the front wheel. We were getting back once more to a serious motorcycle intended for hard riding, as opposed to the cafe racer theme which seemed to have crept in for a while. The tank panel changed to red and the Trident nameplate on the side panel also had a red background.

By 1974 production of the Trident had been moved in its entirety to the BSA works at Small Heath, Birmingham after extensive re-tooling, thanks to the Meriden blockade. Once again the colour changed to Gold and Black and the compression ratio came down from 9 to 8.25 to 1.

Finally, in 1975, major changes were made in what was to be the last of the line, the T160. Most noticeable was the employment of the sloping cylinder engine, previously used on the Rocket 3 (now discontinued). A five-speed gearbox and Trident-style timing and gearbox end covers ensured a genuine Triumph appearance. Foot controls were changed over, gearchange on the left and brake on the right, to meet American legislation. An electric starter was squeezed in behind the cylinders which, being sloped, gave a little more space. Four exhaust pipes swept down below the engine where they mysteriously

merged into two and thence into two megaphone-type silencers. The rear drum brake was replaced by a 10 inch disc as at the front and a rather pleasant curvaceous tank at last replaced the slab-sided design of 1968. Finish was red and white,

with a yellow option for America. This was the last Trident of all and production ceased before the year (1975) was out.

Race Results with the BSA/Triumph 'Threes'

Date	Circuit	Event	Machine	Result
14/3/70	Daytona (USA)	AMA 750	F750	2 & 3
23/5/70	NW 200	Production	Production	1 & 2
6/6/70	I.O.M.	Production TT	Production	1
8/8/70	Brands Hatch	Hutchinson 100	F750	2
12-13/9/70	Montlhery	Bol d'Or 24 Hr	Prod	1
20/9/70	Mallory Park	Race of the Year	F750	3 & 4
4/10/70	Brands Hatch	"Daytona Race"	F750	1, 2 & 3
13/3/71	Oulton Park	British Championship	F750	1
14/3/71	Daytona (USA)	AMA 750	F750	1 & 2
28/3/71	Thruxton	British Championship	F750	1 & 2
9/4/71	Brands Hatch	British Championship	F750	2
9/5/71	Thruxton	500 Mile	Prod	1 & 2
30/5/71	Mallory Park	British Championship	F750	1
5/6/71	I.O.M.	F750 TT	F750	1 & 2
6/6/71	I.O.M.	Production TT	Production	1, 2 & 3
11/7/71	Snetterton	British Championship	F750	1 & 2
8/8/71	Brands Hatch	Hutchinson 100	F750	1 & 2
22/8/71	Silverstone	F750	F750	1 & 2
22/8/71	Silverstone	Production	Prod	1, 2 & 3
4/9/71	Castle Coombe	British Championship	F750	1
11-12/9/71	Montlhéry	Bol d'Or 24 Hr	Prod	1
19/9/71	Mallory Park	Race of the Year	F750	1. 2 & 3
3/10/71	Brands Hatch	Race of the South	F750	1
17/10/71	Ontario (USA)	CMA 750	F750	1 & 2 (leg 1)
17/10/71	Ontario (USA)	CMA 750	F750	1 (leg 2)
1972	Works support was withdrawn in 1972 but bikes were loaned to one or two riders on a 'pay your own expenses' basis and the success story continued, wins being recorded in many events including the Anglo-American Match Races, the Production TT, the F750 TT and the Superbike Championship.			

SPECIFICATION

Technical data

Note: Three sets of figures are quoted here for comparison. The first and last T150 models and the final T160.

	1968	1974/5	1975
Model number	T150	T150V	T160
Engine type	ohv	ohv	ohv
No of cylinders	3	3	3
Bore/stroke mm	67/70	67/70	67/70
Capacity cc	740	740	740
Compression ratio	9.5	8.25	9.5
Engine sprocket teeth	28	28	23
Clutch sprocket teeth	50	50	43
Gearbox sprocket teeth	19	18	19
Rear wheel sprocket teeth	52	50	50
Rpm @ 10 mph (top gear)	657	668	655
Gear ratios 5th	–	4.98	4.92
4th	4.89	5.93	5.85
3rd	5.83	6.97	6.89
2nd	8.3	9.16	9.05
1st	11.95	12.90	12.72
Carburetters	Amal (3)	Amal (3)	Amal (3)
Carburetter type	Concentric	Concentric	Concentric
Primary chain size in.	$\frac{3}{8}$ Triplex	$\frac{3}{8}$ Triplex	$\frac{7}{16}$ Duplex
Rear chain size in.	$\frac{5}{8}$ x $\frac{3}{8}$	$\frac{5}{8}$ x $\frac{3}{8}$	$\frac{5}{8}$ x $\frac{3}{8}$
Tyre size front in.	3.25 x 19	4.10 x 19	4.10 x 19
Tyre size rear in.	4.10 x 19	4.10 x 19	4.10 x 19
Front brake diam in. (mm)	8 (20.32)	10 (252)	10 (252)
Front brake type	2LS	Disc	Disc
Rear brake diam in. (mm)	7 (178)	7 (178)	10 (252)
Rear brake type	1LS	1LS	Disc
Finish	Aquamarine	Gold/Black	Red/Ivory
Seat height in. (mm)	32 (813)	$31\frac{1}{2}$ (800)	$31\frac{1}{2}$ (800)
Wheelbase in. (mm)	$56\frac{1}{4}$ (1429)	58 (1473)	58 (1473)
Length in. (mm)	$86\frac{3}{4}$ (2203)	88 (2235)	88 (2235)
Width in. (mm)	$28\frac{1}{2}$ (724)	29 (736)	29 (736)
Ground clearance in. (mm)	$6\frac{1}{2}$ (165)	$6\frac{1}{2}$ (165)	$6\frac{1}{2}$ (165)
Dry weight lb. (kilo)	470 (213)	462 (209)	493 (225)
Fuel Imp gal (litre)	$4\frac{1}{4}$ (19.14)	$4\frac{1}{2}$ (20.4)	$4\frac{1}{2}$ (20.4)
Oil pints (litre)	6 (3.35)	5.8 (3.3)	5.8 (3.3)

T150V

Engine	740cc vertical transverse three cylinder ohv. Alloy cylinder head and die cast alloy block. Three Amal Concentric carburetters, flexibly mounted. Overhead valves operated from two gear driven camshafts. Three contact breakers. Dry sump lubrication with high capacity gear type oil pump. Separate rubber mounted oil tank and oil cooler.
Gearbox	Five speeds, built in unit with the engine. Single dry plate diaphragm clutch. Positive footchange right-hand side.
Electrical & Lighting Equipment	12 volt. One coil per cylinder. Crankshaft mounted alternator. Master electrical switch. Direction indicators.
Fuel Tank	All steel welded, with quick release filler cap. Rubber knee grips and plated name panel.
Frame	Heavy duty brazed cradle frame with single front down tube.
Forks	Polished aluminium sliders with two-way damping. Protective rubber gaiters.
Rear Suspension	Swinging fork hydraulically damped and adjustable for load.
Wheels	Plated spokes and rims. Dunlop tyres.
Brakes	Triumph/Lockheed hydraulic single disc front brake. Rear drum brake. Light alloy hubs.
Silencers	Large capacity megaphone style, heavily plated.
Twinseat Assembly	Well upholstered seat of ample size for rider and passenger. Hinged for easy access to electrical equipment.
Handlebar	Comfortably shaped bar and control levers, all chromium plated. Nylon lined clutch cable.

T150

Principal visual differences on this earlier model were:- 8 inch diameter twin leading shoe front brake. Silencers with three short tail pipes. Black enamelled sliders to front forks. Enclosed rear suspension springs. Enamelled mudguards. Mechanically, the major difference was a four-speed gearbox.

T160

Many visual changes in this final Trident. More traditional bulbous tank shape. Forward sloping cylinder block. Gearchange pedal on left-hand side, footbrake on right. 10 inch disc brake replaces old 7 inch drum on rear wheel. Silencer shape modified. Four exhaust pipes sweep under engine to a collector box, thence to two silencers. Mechanically, the most significant difference from the earlier models is the provision of an electric starter.

ROAD TESTS
BY JOHN ROBINSON

■ I'd forgotton what it was like to bike British, as NVT's ads are now exhorting us all to do. So much so that the T160 came as something as a shock to my Jap-coddled system. Something like diving into a cold pool, wondering why you hadn't the sense to dip a toe in first when, suddenly, it doesn't seem so bad after all.

■ Half way through Day One of the test I was wondering why I'd jumped in at all and not sat by the edge basking in the Japanese sunshine. By about Day Four I'd become a confirmed non-swimmer!

■ But the Trident grows on you. My only regret now is that it took so long to re-appreciate it and get into the subtleties which can't be pictured or described in a mere few pages. It finally came home to me on the last day of the test, in a frantic dash back to Andover to return the bike before the factory locked up for the night. The Trident is a very usable and very nimble motorcycle.

The electric start model has been on the books for a couple of years now, being announced to the world in general when a film crew, covering the early days of the Meriden business, caught Doug Hele saying he wanted to pick up some starter motors for the T160. The model has been long overdue and most of the changes that have taken place should have been built into the early machines. I'm certain that today's market would be very different if there had been an electric start, disc-braked Trident to compete with the Honda fours.

We're told that there are a couple of hundred changes in the new model, most of them being minor details, compliances with US regulations and off-shoots from the more radical changes. There's the starter motor, of course, and a bigger battery to cope with it, plus six-volt, ballast resistor ignition coils. When the starter is switched on the resistors are cut out putting full battery voltage across the coils. The idea is to compensate for the voltage drop caused by the motor, ensuring that there is enough power to feed the ignition. This and the left-hand gearshift forced a redesign of the crankcase castings.

The barrels tip forward at 15 degrees, like the BSA motors, which although done for other reasons, helps the styling a lot. The ingenuity of the redesigned castings demonstrates to what lengths NVT will go to avoid anything as nasty as a horizontally split motor. The three - into - four - into - two exhaust system smacks of a high level of badge engineering. They may say it was the easiest way of maintaining power and reducing noise, but it's very easy to claim anything you like about exhaust systems.

Fitting the rear disc brake is a much more logical step, not because it's any better than a drum but because it has got to be cheaper and easier for a works already fitting front discs. Especially when you learn that the front and rear discs are interchangeable. And it is something the Japanese haven't got around to yet, except Honda's Gold Wing.

The only other structural change, as it were, is the "short" frame, as fitted to the works production racers and homogated as phase two frames before things dried up. The lower frame tubes have been hoisted up, giving more angle of lean clearance, the front fork movement shortened and the swinging arm lengthened. The nett result is to preserve the original wheelbase of 58 inches but with a significant change in weight distribution. The steering head bearings are adjustable taper rollers.

I'm in two minds about the styling. From some angles it looks good, from others it looks cumbersome, particularly the top of the big tank. The T160 feels heavy and cumbersome too, mainly because when parked on the prop stand it leans over more than usual, requiring a fair effort to get it up on to its feet. Once moving, though, the weight seems to be on your side giving the machine a substantial and very steady feel.

When I first climbed into the seat the Trident felt very wide, an impression which may have been exaggerated as I'd just spent a lot of time on some very slender trail bikes. It was another of those things which I gradually got used to. My only lasting criticism has the seat which felt as if the foam just squashed down to the hard, flat platform below and got painful after riding for a couple of hours. The riding position, while not being bad, wasn't exactly right, either. The angle of the handlebars didn't suit me and the footrest would be better just a couple of inches further back.

The T160 fires up with a deep rumble and only needed the minimum of warming, although we were blessed with warm weather all the way through the test. It doesn't have that immediate, powerful surge associated with Commandos, Bonnevilles and big twins in general, but it builds up smoothly with a lot more thrust at the top end. It has the same effortless qualities, being slightly deceptive, to use that good old, well-worn phrase, in that it never appears to be going that rapidly and doesn't need constant effort from the rider.

Gear-shifting is one of the small but welcome improvements which alone has made the switch from right to left worthwhile. Not that it's any better for being on the opposite side but while NVT were at it they removed the Triumph click and generally made the whole thing sweeter. And there are five ratios to play with.

On the road the Trident is stable in a very solid sort of way. High speed bumps get past the suspension and if you don't see them coming in time to take the jolt through the footrests it gets uncomfortable. While I found the riding position unnatural it was reasonably good in heavy traffic and to my surprise was OK at high speed, at least as far as wind pressure and strain on the arms was concerned.

It was probably because I had to get used to the riding position that it took time to explore the Trident's handling abilities. The neutral feel, combined with the bulk don't add up to the fine response or the feedback that you get from, say, a big Ducati. It copes with bumps better when it is cranked over than when it is upright and the only time it caught me off-guard was when it reacted more than I'd expected to a fairly strong cross-wind. A day at the test track showed that it was, if anything, better than I'd supposed. At the track we discovered it could be run increasingly harder through the turns and its behaviour actually got better. We also discovered that the speedo was near enough accurate.

Lack of handling feedback showed up at the track, when in the early stages a rider following the T160 came into the paddock to say that it was leaving black lines through a couple of the corners. I then found that about a quarter of an inch of rubber was missing from the left

Still unmistakably a Triumph the T160 now boasts Norton Commando silencers as well as the long awaited electric starter. Below: More footrest rubber being stuck to the road by Robinson!

BIKING BRITISH

footrest but I hadn't felt a thing. When we went out again the only way I noticed the grounding was to push my toes out to the end of the footrest. At the end of the day the Trident had been dragging the left rest through all the turns and had worn a large chunk out of it, while the right rest had only been grazing the floor. This seemed rather curious until I read through NVT's specs and found that the clearance on the left is 39 degrees with the suspension one-third flattened and 41 degrees on the other side. Come to think of it, it still seems curious!

There are plenty of places around the circuit where handling flaws soon show up but the Trident rode serenely through all of them, being hampered only by the left footrest which was making it run wide on a tight left-hander. The odd thing was that there was still no tendency for this to dig in or lift the machine. It was also unusual in its behaviour over the test hill where most machines get airborne. The hill is approached by a long right-hander going down through a dip which gives the suspension plenty to think about, straightening up over the hill. At the bottom, on the far side, lies a left hand hairpin, making it a favourite place to watch strangers to the circuit. The T160 was getting into third half-way through the right hander and taking power all the way through.

It says a lot that such a heavy machine would hold a tight line following the kerb. At the bottom of the dip it moved sideways this presumably being where the right footpeg left its mark, but at this point even the sweet handling Ducati 860GT we tested recently was moving considerably out to the left. By then it was almost peak-

ing in third, just holding its own against the hill.

At the top, instead of lifting, the front wheel tracked all the way over and the back wheel went light. There was a brief surge of revs, then squeals and hops as the brakes caught it and dragged it down into the hairpin. There is a nasty feeling of uncertainty getting a machine into a low gear under very heavy braking and heeling it hard over before it has had a fair chance to stabilise itself. The Trident obviously didn't like standing on its nose from 70-odd mph to be hustled into a hairpin but the TT100s bit into the road and the bike went through without even a twitch. That's how much the Trident keeps in reserve.

The brakes, back and front, are powerful without being sudden or coming on too strong. The front one lost a fair amount of grip on the track after it had got hot, it also developed a nasty squeal and at low speeds the pads could be heard clicking away. It's possible that dirt or grease had got on to the disc or that one pad was sticking instead of floating properly but quite obviously all was not well. The back brake was a lot better than I'd expected, with the right amount of leverage and feel to it. Of course it would lock the wheel, virtually any back brake will, the important thing is that is was controllable, with none of the sogginess or harshness that are often found in hydraulic lines.

There were one or two niggling points about the machine which may or may not be typical. I get tired of having to make allowances for sub-standard test machines but we've done it for other manufacturers and it would be unfair to single NVT out for special criticism. The T160 had a lot of vibration, mainly through the footrests under acceleration. Much of this disappeared after adjusting the final drive chain but there was still some there — a 120-degree three ought to be smoother

than a straight four. The Lucas switches aren't difficult to use but look a bit utilitarian and I wonder how they will stand up to prolonged wet weather. The horn cum flasher button is too small and the flasher part of it didn't work when I collected the model. The neutral indicator light usually came on several seconds after slipping into neutral.

After the initial run up from Andover to London both exhausts were smoking freely and four hundred miles later the tank took a whole pint of oil. A Norton man made the point, which I accept, that the piston rings specified originally for the T160 were not up to the job and had since been changed. Apparently someone decided to use up the remaining stocks or something, and because they wanted to get demonstrators out to the press as early as possible there was a good chance that ours had duff rings.

That, no doubt accounts for the machine's top speed of about 110 flat on the tank and 104 sitting up. NVT say that they look for about 118 mph from the Trident — near enough peak in top — which I'd be prepared to accept.

Finally, when we came to run our acceleration tests, the all metal clutch let go. Dumping it close to peak revs on the first run was more than it could take. Being gentle on the next two runs still produced slip as the motor got up to about 6000. There weren't enough tools in the tool kit to even adjust the cable, let alone the clutch release, so no acceleration curve appears in our performance chart.

If a subjective idea of acceleration is any substitute, I would expect the T160 to turn in a standing quarter in the low to middle thirteens, marginally slower than the 2A Commando mainly because the Norton was so fast (and so easy) off the line.

Even though our top speed was possibly under par, there's enough power there and an ample rev margin to cruise at 90-plus and the T160 seems well within its limits at this sort of speed. Reliability was one thing which never bugged Doug

Hele's racers and ought to be one of the T160's strongest selling points.

No doubt Triumph's race development taught them a lot about the threes but one thing is sadly lacking — the beautiful sound. It's still in there only the efficient Norton silencers won't let it out. Certainly the rider never hears it over the wind rush.

British industry has nearly caught up with the Japanese when it comes to fuel consumption — is the gallon getting smaller or the mile getting longer? — on a 70 mph motorway run the Trident did 40 mpg, dropping to 35 mpg at the test track. Ours had the big, 4.8 gallon tank which should give it a range approaching 190 miles, except that it kept running on to reserve about 112 miles after filling the tank — are there 2 gallons in reserve or did we really have the small 3.7 gallon job?

NVT have now found themselves in the slightly awkward position of having what amounts to two first-generation superbikes to sell in a crowded market. They intend to resolve this by giving the T160 the sporty image and packaging the Norton as Britain's grand tourer. According to their specifications both turn out 58 bhp, as did the early Trident, the Norton doing it at 5900 while the T160 steams all the way up to 7250 with a safe limit of 8000. The Trident is also £54 more expensive, at £1215 and about 40lb heavier. Obviously, the sports versus tourer decision was not taken lightly.

The price puts it in the same league as, er, well the Norton, the 600 BMW, the Ducati V-twins, the Z1 Kawasaki and the rotary Suzuki. The unfortunate thing is that the closest competitors are really the Honda and Suzuki 750s, as far as volume sales go, and both of these are much cheaper.

The T160 will certainly appeal to those who like their motorcycling fast and rugged. I can't help feeling, though, that it still needs a little extra something to make it stand out from the crowd — NVT almost got there with the JP replica and the earlier Vetter-styled three.

MOTOR CYCLE MECHANICS

ENGINE

type	OHV in-line three
displacement	740 ccm
bore x stroke	67 x 70 mm
compression ratio	9.5:1
claimed output	58 bhp at 7250 rpm
lubrication	dry sump
carburettors	three 27 mm Amal
ignition	contact breaker and coil
charging/lighting	12V ac/dc, 120W alternator feeding battery via rectifier and Zener diode

TRANSMISSION

clutch	single plate, diaphragm spring
primary drive	duplex chain
gear ratios	12.72; 9.05; 6.89; 5.85; 4.92
final drive	chain
engine sprocket	23T
clutch sprocket	43T
gearbox sprocket	19T (17 to 23T available)
wheel sprocket	50T

CHASSIS

front tyre	4.10 x 19 Dunlop
rear tyre	4.10 x 19 Dunlop
front suspension	two-way damped tele fork
rear suspension	swing arm with Girling dampers
front brake	10 inch hydraulic disc
rear brake	10 inch hydraulic disc
wheelbase	58 inch
castor	62 degrees
overall length	88 inch
overall width	29 inch
seat height	31 inch
dry weight	503 lb
test weight	525 lb
tank capacity	4.8 gallon or 3.7 gallon
oil tank capacity	6 pints

PARTS PRICES (inc. VAT)

front mudguard	£9.97
handlebar	£7.75
speedo cable	£2.52
exhaust system	£109.26
set of points	£1.30
set of pistons	£19.70
list price	£1,215
warranty	6 months or 6,000 miles including parts and labour.
manufacturer	Norton Triumph Europe Ltd., North Way, Walworth Industrial Estate, Andover, Hants.

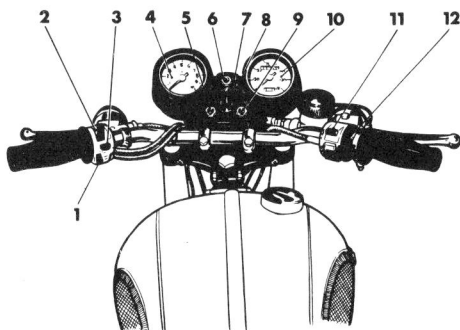

1, Horn/flasher. 2. Dip switch. 3. Indicator switch. 4, RPM x 1000
5, Main beam indicator. 6, Flasher indicator. 7, Neutral indicator.
8, Ignition key. 9, Ignition indicator. 10, Speedometer with trip.
11, Starter button. 12, Engine kill button.

TEST CONDITIONS

overcast, dry
ambient temperature 60 deg F
wind gusting 10-15 mph.

PERFORMANCE

maximum speed	110 mph
braking from 30 mph	30 feet
fuel consumption	
hard riding	35 mpg
average	38 mpg
minimum speeds in gears	
1st	6 mph
2nd	9 mph
3rd	11 mph
4th	13 mph
5th	16 mph

mph 1000 rpm in top 15.1
speedo error
1 mph fast at true 70 mph

HOW IT COMPARES

MODEL	Price inc. VAT	Max Speed	Average mpg	SS ¼ mile	Dry Weight lbs
Trident T160	£1,215	110*	38	not taken*	503
Ducati 860GT	1,299	110	42	13.2	452
Kawasaki Z1 900	1,249	135	48	12.3	506
Suzuki RE5	1,195	105	33	14.5	507
Honda 750 4	979	112	49	13.0	480
Norton Commando Mk. 2A 830cc	928	110	50	12.5	410

*See text for further information

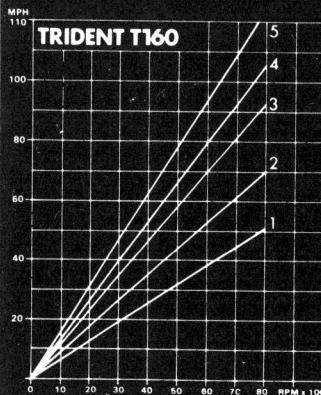

TRIDENT T160

TRIDENT T160

Motor Cycle News

Trident

THE STORY BEHIND THE TRIUMPH-3

THREE years ago, Doug Hele and Bert Hopwood of Triumph's development staff, got together and roughed out some designs for the Triumph of the future. The Trident was born a three-cylinder design based on the well-tried T100 unit, with a completely different bore and stroke — 67 mm × 70 mm against the T100's 69 mm × 65.5 mm.

The eventual three-cylinder unit retains much of the twin look about it, but the third pot gives it much better torque and smoothness, and revs safely to 8,000 revs per minute.

The 120° crank is mounted on four main bearings in a three-way-split crankcase. A horizontal car-type split case was considered but dropped because of oil leak problems.

With the third cylinder, three times more oil has to be circulated as with the 650 twins.

This produced cooling problems which have been overcome by the oil radiator under the petrol tank.

Two camshafts are mounted at the front and back of the crankcases as on the twins but mounted in three plain bearings. These, the main bearings and the rocker gear, are all pressure-fed with oil.

The cylinders are a one-piece alloy casting with steel liner inserts. The cylinder head is also alloy with triple rubber-mounted Amal concentric carburetters. An alloy cast beam with three arms operates the three slides direct, with one cable going to the twist grip.

The 12 volt alternator is now housed in the timing cover and

works off the end of the crank while the set of triple points are driven from the end of the camshaft.

The gearbox internals are very similar to the 650 twins but a massive triplex chain now drives a car-type single plate diaphragm clutch, manufactured by Lockheed to cope with the 60 b.h.p. The primary chain is tensioned by twin slipper-type tensioners in the chaincase.

The frame is similar to the Bonneville with a single downtube, but the Trident version is about an inch longer and has thicker tubing.

NEW TYRES

The exhaust has undergone considerable development for maximum efficiency. The middle exhaust splits and siameses into the two outer pipes.

To cope with the extra weight and power, Dunlop developed new tyres based on the triangular racing covers. Both front and rear rims have massive 4·10×19 covers, type KR81.

Speedometer and rev-counter heads are mounted in rubber together with the ammeter. Drive for the tachometer comes out neatly from the front of the engine, driven by the exhaust camshaft.

General greasing is recommended every 2,000 miles with oil changes every 4,000 — both services quite easy enough for the average owner to carry out himself.

The transverse cylinder layout, exhaust manifold and oil-cooling radiator.

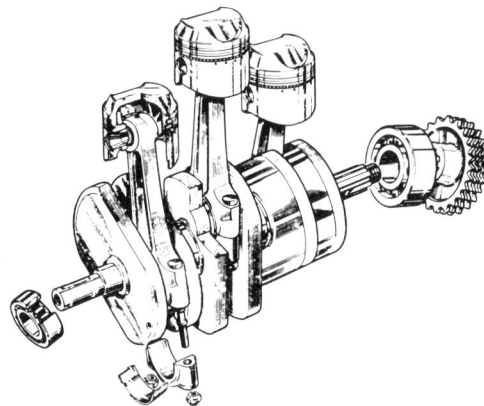

Three-throw crankshaft assembly showing the split big-end bearing and mainshaft bearings.

Neat and surprisingly compact, the Trident shows off its distinct looks. The motor still has some of the Bonneville look about it, while the top half is slightly Honda. Note the oil cooler radiator under the tank.

SPECIFICATION

ENGINE:
Bore and stroke	67 mm 70 mm
Capacity	741 c.c.
Compression ratio	9.5 : 1
Output	60 b.h.p. at 8,000 r.p.m.
Ignition	Battery and three coils
Lighting	12 volt alternator
Carburetters	3 Amal Concentric 626 (27 mm)

TRANSMISSION:
Primary	Triplex ⅜ in. chain
Secondary	⅜ in. ⅜ in. chain
Clutch	Single-plate Lockheed

GEAR RATIOS:
First	11.54 : 1
Second	7.95 : 1
Third	5.6 : 1
Top	4.7 : 1

CAPACITIES:
Petrol	4¼ gallons
Consumption	39.5 m.p.g.
Range	175 miles
Oil	6 pints

WHEELS:
Tyres (front and rear)	4.10 19
Front brake	8 in. 2LS
Rear brake	7 in. SLS

DIMENSIONS:
Weight	482 lbs. (dry)
Seat height	32 in.
Overall length	87 in.
Ground clearance	6½ in.

PERFORMANCE DATA

At Motor Industries Research Association test track at Lindley, Warwickshire.

Rider, in racing leathers, prone on tank.

FROM 40 m.p.h. TOP GEAR ACCELERATION:	East	West	Mean m.p.h.
Terminal speed after ¼ mile	91·10	94·9	92·09
Maximum speeds	123·0	130·0	126·45
Standing quarter terminal speeds	100·5	107·2	103·75

TIMES:			Seconds
Standing quarter	13·9	13·6	13·75
0—60 m.p.h.			5·00

SPEEDOMETER ERROR:
1·1 m.p.h. slow at 40 m.p.h.

REVS:
R.p.m. at 10 m.p.h. in top 684

Flying Trident puts you in the jet-set

by Gavin Trippe

IT'S BEEN rumoured about. It's been whispered about. Now it's arrived. The 750 c.c. Triumph three-cylinder Trident — the most explosive motor-cycle to sear up the highway in two-wheeled history.

With its own unique snarl, it outdrags any production car on the road up to 100 m.p.h. There are two ways of achieving arm-stretching acceleration to the magic "ton" in under 14 seconds after a mere quarter of a mile. Buy a Lamborghini or Ferrari for £8,000, or a Triumph Trident for £540!

Up through the gears to 8,000 r.p.m. with your cheeks pinned back to your ears, the Trident thrusts you back so much, you cannot reach forward to pull in the clutch and grab another gear. And flat on the tank at 130 m.p.h. is something just out of sight and mind. The fastest Manx Nortons in the Isle of Man TT only manage to clock that velocity through MCN's speed trap.

No novelty

The novelty of three cylinders is no gimmick, for the extra pot transforms this monster with hair-raising capabilities into a real smoothy. One prod from the kick-start fires it up and the smooth torque of the motor, even pulling away from 40 m.p.h. in top, is a revelation.

The thrill derived from doing standing starts and feeling that big hand trying to pluck you off the back of the seat is unbelievable. And the distinct exhaust note, unobtrusive as it is, will go down in history along with the Scott "yowl" and the Vincent's "burble."

To handle the 60 b.h.p., Triumph use a single plate Lockheed clutch which totally eliminates Triumph "crunch" as you select bottom and the four-speed gearbox slides through its motions admirably.

Static, the Trident is a bit of a handful. Lifting it on to the centre stand makes muscles ache, but Triumph have managed to get a very low seat height which allows both feet to be planted firmly on the ground at traffic lights.

Once in motion, the Trident seems to shed most of the 480 lbs and becomes a very manageable bike.

The handling is very good with no wander at high speed. It is as steady as the Queen Mary round fast or slow corners. The massive 4·10 - 19 Dunlop KR81 tyres glue it down pretty well, though discretion is the better part of valour in the wet.

The only time it snaked and showed its weight was when I motored over some cats-eyes, but it was never anything to worry about.

The riding position was very good, solo or two up. A rapid two up test left the pillion passenger with knuckles white from anxiously gripping the grab rail.

After a hard thrashing, including the MIRA timing tests, the motor showed no signs of distress. It had no oil leaks, and no adjustments were made. Maintenance is fairly straighforward and everything is relatively easily accessible. But getting the middle sparking plug out with the tank still on is a masterpiece of fiddling.

The electrics are housed under the hinged seat and the rather skimpy toolkit and battery under the left-hand styling side panel.

The looks are quite handsome, with I think the Triumph outshining its B.S.A. Rocket 3 sister.

Fishtails

I didn't go a bundle on those fishtail exhaust pipes and cannot understand why the handlebar layout has not changed since the advent of the first Speed Twin before the war. We still have to put up with clamped-on levers, an ugly pressed steel horn button on one side and cut-out button "twin" on the other, and an air lever.

All the sundry wiring and cables snake their way into the headlight nacelle like spaghetti. Our accessory manufacturers want to have a good look at Japanese cockpit neatness and quality and learn a lesson.

But these are minor quibbles and they don't alter my opinion that this is the greatest bike I have ever had the opportunity to ride.

I once owned a big Vincent and have always been on the verge of buying another for keeps, but if I were to own a motor bike now it would have to be a Trident.

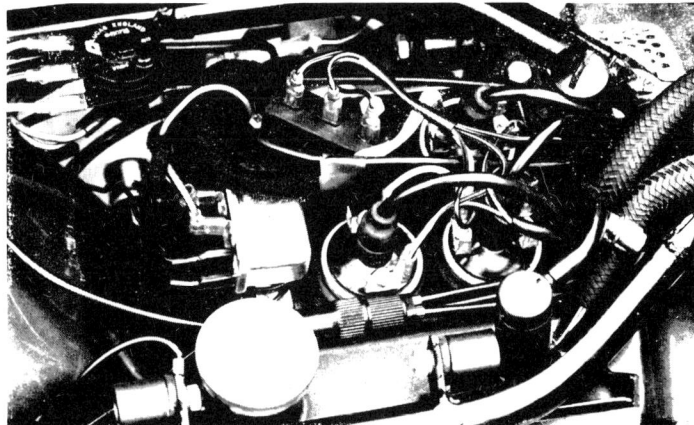

View showing coils and other electrical equipment, all of which is housed under the hinged dual seat.

OWNER'S VIEW

The Trident undoubtedly established its quality and reputation on the race tracks of the world where for quite some time in the early seventies it was supreme in F750 and Production racing. Factories race to influence buyers and successful racing undoubtedly does influence buyers, particularly if the racer bears a close resemblance to its showroom counterpart as in the case of the Trident. This rarely happens in grand prix racing but it does in F750 and production categories and many Trident owners will tell you that the exploits of Tony Jefferies, Paul Smart, Percy Tait, Malcolm Uphill and Ray Pickrell among others, encouraged them to opt for a Triumph three. Being very fast, quite heavy and somewhat expensive in its day, the Trident attracted mature buyers with a lot of experience under their Barbour suits. So in selecting owners to interview, I have three very experienced riders, two of whom are members of the Triumph Owners MCC. and the third owns no less than five Triumphs. First we have Richard Tate, Secretary of the club and based in London. He bought a 1970 T150.

IGD Why did you buy a Trident?
RT The main reason was to get a Triumph with a larger engine and the Trident has the largest one going.

IGD Did you buy new or secondhand?
RT I bought it new.
IGD Any early problems?
RT Well, yes. With only 3 miles on the clock it had to be returned as the oil pump had failed, also whilst this was being done, a suspect clutch was replaced. I was unlucky, I suppose.
IGD What repairs have you done?
RT Once on the road again, no problems until 14,000 miles when I holed a piston. The problem was traced to the contact breaker. Another piston went 3000 miles later. I attributed this to low fuel and high revs. My local dealer carried out the work, although an owner could have done it with suitable service tools.
IGD Have you experienced any difficulty in obtaining parts?
RT No, none whatever. There always seem to be adequate stocks around.
IGD What kind of performance and handling does your machine have?
RT Very good indeed. I always used the machine with a sidecar and it was the only bike I have ever ridden which would hold 100 mph with a sidecar, and do 32 miles to the gallon.
IGD Do you use your machine every day?
RT I did until I sold it in 1979.
IGD How practical was it and were the running costs reasonable?
RT It was a very good sidecar machine and providing one serviced it regularly, the running costs were reasonable, particularly bearing in mind that a sidecar gives a machine a hard time.
IGD When did you join the Triumph Owners MCC. Was it helpful in any way?
RT I joined in 1968 and I would recommend every Triumph owner to join if he wants to get the maximum enjoyment out of his machine. I had no mechanical experience with motorcycles before I joined but I have learned a lot since that time.
IGD Do you have a favourite dealer to turn to?

RT Certainly – Hughes of High Street, Tooting, London.
IGD Did you enjoy your motorcycling on a Trident?
RT Yes, it was definitely the best bike I ever owned, I wish now that I had not sold it.
IGD What advice would you give to potential Trident owners?
RT Never run at high speed with only one fuel tap turned on. Oh! and join the club.

Richard Tate's views on the Trident were brief and to the point but he was obviously a satisfied owner, not dismayed by one or two problems. His enthusiastic endorsement of the Triumph Owners MCC is to be expected seeing that he 'rose through the ranks' to become its General Secretary, an onerous post in such a large organisation.

My next interviewee was Martin Jones, Branch Secretary of the Birmingham and Wolverhampton Branch of the club, and he goes into some detail.
IGD When did you buy a Trident?
MJ I bought my machine, a T150V, new in May 1975, having fancied one since I first saw the works testers running back and forth to MIRA in the 60s. It was the unique sound that got my attention.
IGD What repairs have been necessary?
MJ Having done 103,000 miles in under eight years, some have been necessary. Front wheel bearings were poorly protected and needed renewal every six months or so. This was cured by fitting rubber sealed bearings. The bottom head bearings also wore quickly. They are exposed and winter salt turns them rusty. Norman Hyde suggests that dirt is blown up the front down tube which is open at the bottom. I'll try blocking that up next. The motor was rebored at 59,000 miles and I rebuilt the bottom end at 86,000. The gearbox hardly needed touching, not even any marks on the teeth or dogs.
IGD Any difficulty with parts?
MJ No, in the West Midlands we have Vale Onslow's, Bob Joiner,

Bennetts and Autocycle. If the first one had not got what I wanted one of the others had.

IGD How about performance?

MJ Very satisfactory for fast long distance touring.

IGD Do you use the machine every day?

MJ Yes, it tends to get lumpy in heavy town traffic but is fine on the open road.

IGD Are your running costs reasonable?

MJ It tends to get through chains and rear tyres at a fair rate but is otherwise moderate.

IGD Have you won any prizes in concours or similar events?

MJ I have won a couple of times in concours events run by my branch but I have never entered any national events.

IGD When did you join the Triumph Owners MCC? Would you recommend other Triumph owners to join?

MJ I joined in May 1977 and am now Branch Secretary. It is a handy forum for discussing problems and others will always have an answer if you cannot think of one. One can also make good contacts with those working in allied trades and the store of knowledge available is very useful. Definitely worthwhile to join.

IGD Do you have a favourite dealer to turn to for your work or do you do it yourself? If the latter, what special tools are necessary?

MJ No, I do all my own work. It is basically a very simple engine to work on and only two special tools are imperative. One is the camshaft timing pinion extractor and the other is the clutch centre extractor. Apart from these, you need a garage and a good set of socket and ring spanners and a torque wrench.

IGD How would you sum up the enjoyment you get from your machine?

MJ I get enjoyment from touring and camping and the regular trips abroad. Also a fair amount of fast motorway riding. It is the longest I have ever kept one bike and I would

seriously consider keeping it, even if I did get another.

IGD A satisfied owner! What advice would you give to potential owners of the Trident?

MJ If you look after the oil and the oil filter, the engine will look after itself. Despite the high mileage, my crank has not needed regrinding and the gearbox seems bullet proof. It is possible that some credit for this could go to the Molyslip additives I put in the oils.

IGD Any other comments?

MJ Lucas RITA gives the engine amazing flexibility with power coming in at 2000 rpm rather than 4500, and 50 mpg for all-round riding which is very good compared with tales of 35 mpg from other owners. RITA gives a huge deep blue spark which must give the engine much better combustion. I tried the Boyer system but whilst this gave good starting, it was not too reliable. For the best handling I fit an 18 inch rear wheel with a 4.25 Road Runner and an Avon Venom on the front with a WM3 rim.

The most unusual looking three cylinder Triumph (some would call it bizarre by Triumph standards) is undoubtedly the Hurricane or X75, produced in 1975 mainly for sale in the United States where the styling originated. Only a limited number were built and I anticipated some difficulty in finding one in UK let alone almost on my doorstep, which is what actually happened. Enquiries around the local dealers and suppliers soon enabled me to locate Daniel Keith Evans in the village of Bishops Tachbrook, just outside Leamington Spa. Dan, I discovered, is a diesel technician at the local Ford distributor and when he opened his lock-up door to show me the Hurricane, I was somewhat astonished to find that he owned a fleet of Triumphs, for in addition to the Hurricane there were two (yest, two!) T160s, a 750 Trophy Trail and a 500.

The Hurricane was wheeled out and it was obviously in

immaculate condition. I questioned Dan as follows:-

IGD When did you buy this machine, was it new or secondhand and why did you buy it?

DKE I bought it just over a year ago, in November 1982, and it was secondhand. I bought it because it looked like no other Triumph has ever looked and was therefore unique.

IGD What condition was it in, did you have any problems to cope with?

DKE It had been totally rebuilt and apart from a slight oil mist around the head gasket and rocker box base gaskets, it seemed to be in good condition.

IGD What work have you done on it, if any?

DKE All I have done is to replace two rocker box gaskets and pushrod seals.

IGD Have you had any difficulty in getting parts?

DKE I have not needed any cycle parts as yet but Norman Hyde and Les Williams, locally, seem to have most things.

IGD What kind of performance and handling does it have?

DKE It is not really a machine for riding fast and far like the T160, but its performance is average and the handling quite good.

IGD Do you use it every day?

DKE No, it is not really very practical for everyday use and besides, it is in too good condition to expose it to bad weather and salt on the roads in winter.

IGD Have you won any prizes in Concours or similar events?

DKE No, but it was featured in *Classic Bike* on one occasion and also at the Classic Bike Show.

IGD Do you get work done at dealers or do you do it yourself? If the latter, what is needed in the way of special tools etc?

DKE I do not have any work done at dealers, I prefer to do it myself. I go to Norman Hyde or Jack Butler (dealer in Leamington Spa) for advice and they are very helpful. You do need a good tool kit with all the right spanners, piston ring

clamps and a good torque wrench.
IGD How would you sum up the enjoyment of riding your machines?
DKE You get more smiles per mile riding any Triumph motorcycle and there is nothing to beat the sound of a good triple.
IGD What advice would you give to anyone thinking of investing in a Hurricane?
DKE I believe a number of Hurricanes were shipped back from the States and these have probably stood around for a long time over there and parts could be missing or damaged. Only buy this machine if

you have a good garage and another bike as well, as it is too fine a machine to use as daily transport.

At this point Dan kicked up the Hurricane, which started easily, and we both stood listening to that 'sound of a good triple'. He was quite right: there's nothing to beat it! As far as having another bike is concerned, Dan's collection

ensures that he gets plenty of variety on his daily rides and the Hurricane only comes out on special occasions and only then if the sun is shining.

BUYING

The Triumph Trident is a unique British motorcycle with its three cylinders, impressive performance and truly remarkable racing record. In consequence those in search of a good specimen must expect to pay a highish price. The scarcity value also tends to keep the price up, as the machine was only in production for six years and the numbers in no way compared with those of the cheaper twin cylinder models in the range that had been in production for a long time. Another factor which increases the desirability of the Trident, and hence affects the price, is the fact that there is normally little difficulty in getting most replacement parts either from a Triumph dealer or one of the specialist suppliers. Not only are standard parts available but there is now a wide range of special components designed to increase performance, and with these you can convert your standard 750cc engine to a larger capacity — up to 1000cc if you so wish. So it will be seen that the prospective purchaser of a secondhand Trident is fortunate in many ways and is not likely to be beset by the many problems which often occur with older machines long out of production and for which parts are virtually unobtainable.

To anyone not familiar with the Trident but anxious to buy one, a good first move would be to locate the nearest branch of the Triumph Owners club. This is a very big and enthusiastic organisation with branches all over the UK and several overseas. Among the members in your local branch you are bound to find one or more who either runs a Trident or has done in the past and will be only too willing to share his knowledge of the bike with you and even pass judgement on a model which you have located and are considering buying.

Another aspect of the availability of parts is that if your budget is limited you could consider buying a cheap machine in need of overhaul, particularly if you are a good mechanic and have the facilities to do the work. If you lack the facilities and the knowledge, then this route is not for you. However it is comforting to know that there are quite a number of Triumph specialists around who will do the work for you, at a price of course, and such knowledge does not come cheap. However, there are always some jobs that can be done by any averagely knowledgeable motorcyclist and the really difficult stuff can then be left to the experts — this way you will be able to save something and at the same time gain the satisfaction of having done at least some of the work yourself. Cycle parts, for example, should not present too much difficulty as there are plenty of companies around who will undertake beadblasting, plating and enamelling. Wheels and hubs can also be dealt with in this way and replacement tyres and suspension units can be readily obtained. However, when you get to the engine and gearbox, unless you really know what you are doing, pass the whole lot over to an expert. This unit is a big and expensive piece of mechanism and inexpert work followed by a major blow-up could prove disastrous both to one's self esteem and one's pocket!

Where possible always buy a machine with a history which can be verified. Here the Triumph Owners MCC can be useful, particularly if the machine being bought is owned by a club member. Their enthusiasm knows no bounds and you will probably get a day by day history of the bike back to the time it came off the production line! Joking apart, it is better to buy this way than through the small ads in the local paper or at an auction. In the latter case beware of being carried away in the heat of the bidding and finding yourself with a bike whose engine you have not even heard running.

Buying secondhand from an appointed Triumph dealer should obviously be a better move than buying from some completely unknown private owner. With a dealer, he has his reputation to maintain and you can always go back to him in the event of trouble. Many Triumph dealers are enthusiasts for the marque themselves and this tends to make them sympathetic in the event of any difficulties arising.

Incidentally, with the demise of the Triumph Engineering Co Ltd you may wonder whether there are any Triumph dealers still around. The answer is that there are, and even though the emphasis of their business has changed to foreign makes, many still retain their interest, and very often their stocks of Triumph parts.

When buying secondhand one would naturally check all the usual things which apply to any vehicle. Noise, smoke, accident damage, rust, brake levers that come right back to the bar, oil leaks, fuel leaks, slack chains, worn tyres and so on, but with the Trident there are a few special items to look out for. These are 1) Examine the underside of the crankcase for signs of welding — this is where broken rods exit! 2) Look carefully at the front down tube of the frame, just above the engine mounting lug; a crack or break here is not unknown — don't buy it. 3) On the T160 check the side stand lug for bending, which sometimes happens. 4) Raise the fork gaiters and inspect the fork stanchions, wear here is very obvious, and finally 5) Examine the brake discs for scoring. They can sometimes be skimmed but, if they have gone too far, replacement can be expensive.

Some notes penned by Martin Jones following his comments in 'Owner's View' might be of interest here. 'If you are buying secondhand, be very careful. Whilst the Trident thrives on hard work, remaining sound and oil tight, it reacts strongly to neglect coupled with unmerciful thrashing, and unfortunately it seems to attract this kind of owner if the horror stories I've heard from those who

have bought secondhand are anything to go by. If you end up with a bike in this state, the best bet is a total strip down and rebuild to make a fresh start. If you run it in wisely and stay on top of maintenance schedules thereafter you should have no more trouble. It is possible that every 25/30,000 miles you will hear what sounds like severe main bearing failure, but if you open the throttle the noise will stop! In fact what has

happened is that the cush drive rubbers in the clutch have crushed and the vanes are knocking together. If the primary case is removed and the front is taken off the cush drive unit, the rubbers can be replaced with the unit in situ.'

CLUBS, SPECIALISTS & BOOKS

Clubs

There is only one club which caters specifically for Triumph owners and that is the **Triumph Owners Motor Cycle Club**, which has been referred to several times on earlier pages. This club was founded many years ago and has nearly forty branches in the UK as well as several overseas in Australia, New Zealand, France, Spain and USA. The present secretary is Richard Tate, himself a one-time Trident owner who contributes his experiences in this book. The patron of the club is John Nelson, who served many years at Meriden as head of the Experimental Department and later as Service Manager. The club issues a nicely printed magazine every month which keeps members informed of what is going on in the branches and provides a useful forum for members to exchange views on Triumph matters. Technical advice is also given. The magazine is called *Nacelle,* a tribute to that classic example of Edward Turner's styling which cleaned up the handlebar area for so many years until it became unfashionable. Full information about the club and its programme can be obtained from the secretary.:-

Richard Tate
27, Salehurst Road
Crofton Park
London SE4 1AS
(Tel 01-690-5669)

Books

The Trident features in a number of books about Triumph which have been published in recent years. These include:-

It's a Triumph by Ivor Davies published by Haynes/Foulis in 1980 and reprinted in 1982. 237 pages with over 300 photographs from Triumph archives, including Trident racing shots.

The Story of Triumph Motorcycles by Harry Louis and Bob Currie, published by Patrick Stephens Ltd in 1975. 128 pages with black and white photographs and 'exploded' drawings of several Triumph engines, including the Trident.

Triumph Twins & Triples by Roy Beacon published by Osprey Publishing Ltd in 1981. 192 pages, many black and white photographs and detailed specifications from pre-war to 1980.

Whatever Happened to the British Motorcycle Industry? by Bert Hopwood. Written by the man who was largely responsible for the existence of the Trident and telling his story of it in detail. 315 pages, many black & white photographs including prototypes. Published by Haynes/Foulis in 1981.

Triumph Trident Owners Workshop Manual by Frank Meek, covering the Trident T150 models and BSA Rocket 3 Model A75 1969/72. Published by Haynes.

Workshop Manuals, Handbooks, Charts etc, genuine Triumph publications from JR Technical Publications Ltd, Potterdike House, Lombard Street, Newark, Notts NG24 1XG Tel (0636) 71221

Specialists

Norman Hyde
Rigby Close
Heathcote Industrial Estate
Warwick Tel (0926) 497375
Ex Development Engineer, Triumph Eng. Co Ltd. Designer and supplier of many specialist parts for Triumph twins and triples.

Les Williams
Common Lane Industrial Estate
Kenilworth, Warwickshire
Tel (0926) 54948
Ex-Triumph race shop manager. Owner and tuner of 'Slippery Sam', builds replicas and other specials for sale. Trident rebuilds, parts and service.

Other suppliers of Triumph parts and service can be found in the advertisement columns of the motorcycle press.

PHOTO
GALLERY

1

1 & 2.   Two interesting photographs of a prototype
Trident dating back possibly to late 1967 or early 1968.
The oil cooler appears to be enclosed in a box with air
scoops, and there is provision for a tacho drive on the
crankcase nearside. Neither of these items went into
production in this form. The bars are US style and the
controls simple, no flashers or other complications.

2

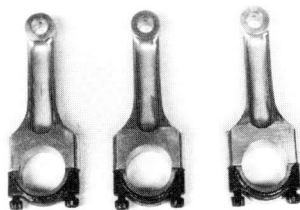

3 & 4. Two very glamorous phoographs of the re-styled T150 taken in the early seventies. Note the conical hubs, the skimpy front guards, the 'pushed back' headlamp with its slender brackets and the 'slimline' forks. The lower one is the American version with the traditional Triumph tank; American customers rejected the original shape, but it continued for other markets.

5. The Trident crankshaft which, after initial forging, is reheated and twisted to provide the 120 degree throws.

6. Forged light alloy connecting rods ...

7. .... and pistons to go with them.

8. Two camshafts as on the twins, mounted high up to keep pushrods short.

9. Massive aluminium alloy cylinder block with pressed-in steel liners spigoted deep into the crankcase.

10. The cylinder block from above.

11. The cylinder head fitted to the X75 Hurricane has wider fins, as can be seen here (right hand photograph).

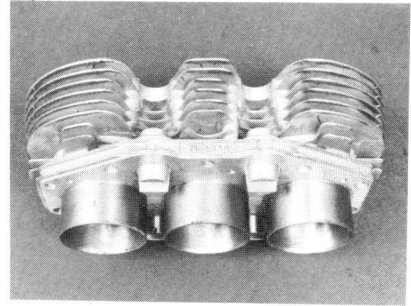

9

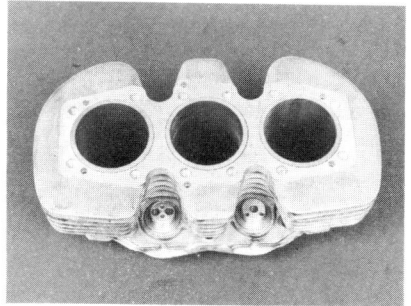

7

8

10

11

12. Cylinder head from above, typical Triumph symmetry.

13. The Borg and Beck diaphragm clutch designed to cope with Trident power.

14. Right-hand side of the T160 engine-gear unit. Note the oil cooler, top right, and the electric starter just above the gearbox.

12

13

14

15. Close-up of the electric starter with its protective cover.

16. Three cylinders, four exhaust pipes, merging into two under the crankcase, oil cooler above.

17. Nearside view of the oil cooler with its end cunningly covered with a side reflector.

18. Impressive bank of carburetters, one for each cylinder, all rubber mounted.

19

20

21

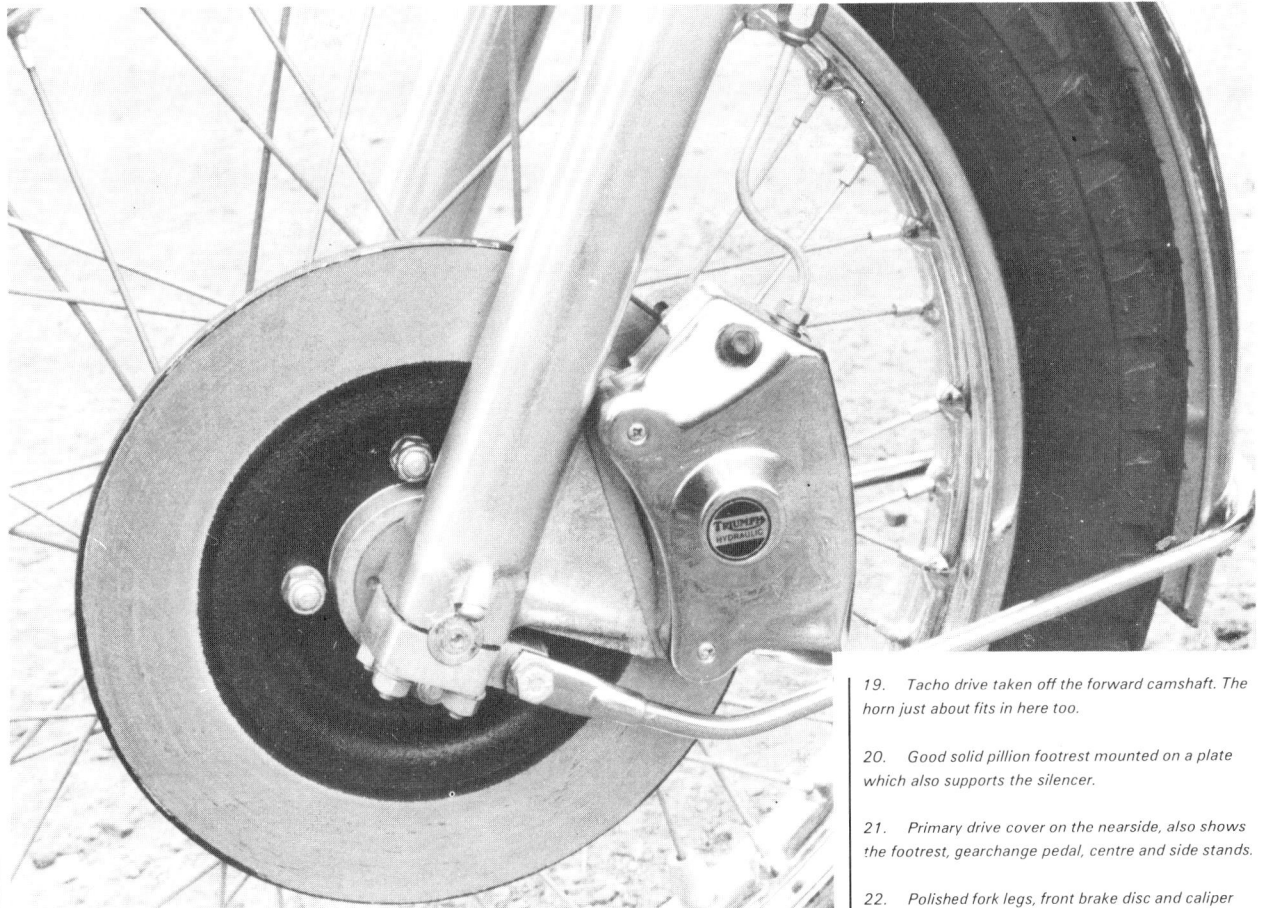

22

19.   Tacho drive taken off the forward camshaft. The horn just about fits in here too.

20.   Good solid pillion footrest mounted on a plate which also supports the silencer.

21.   Primary drive cover on the nearside, also shows the footrest, gearchange pedal, centre and side stands.

22.   Polished fork legs, front brake disc and caliper unit.

23

24

23.　Rear wheel spindle mounting, rear chain and its adjuster. The speedometer drive can just be seen below the fork end.

24.　T160 back-end with upswept silencer, rear brake disc and caliper and suspension unit with its plated spring.

25

26

27

28

25. T160 instruments, headlamp and flashers, an impressive amount of gleaming metal everywhere.

26. Rear electrics and grab handle, all with good solid mountings.

27. Ball ended clutch lever dip switch, horn button and flasher control on the left handlebar.

28. Ball-ended front brake lever, twist grip throttle, electric starter switch and 'kill' button on the right handlebar.

29. T160 back-end. Nicely upholstered seat of ample length, rear brake disc, suspension unit and tail light cluster.

30. Hinged seat on T160. Reveals the oil filler, battery and brake master cylinder. There is also a small space for tools.

29

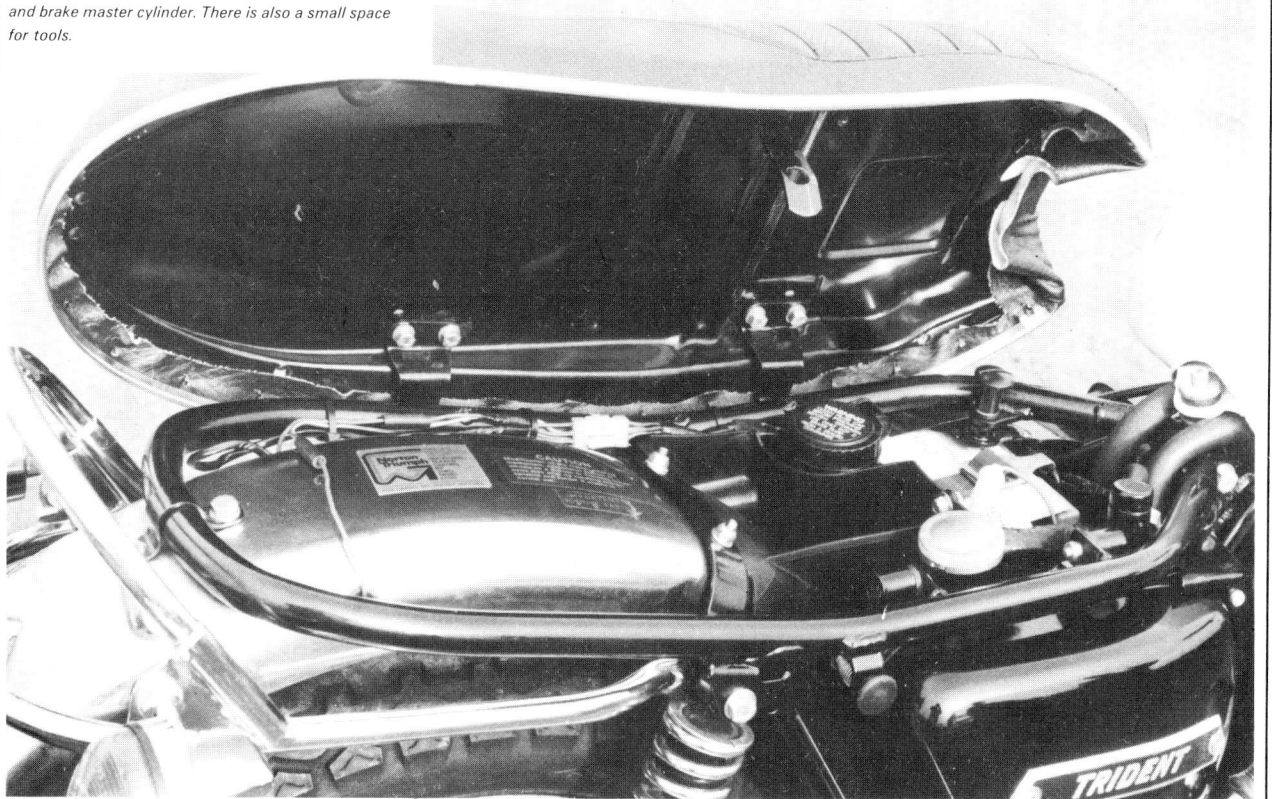

30

31

31. On the X75 Hurricane the seat lifts right off after unscrewing two knobs, one on each side. They look like steering damper knobs!

32. A superb piece of styling on the Les Williams 'Legend' version of the Trident. Clean and purposeful with no gimmickry.

33. Examine the underside of the crankcase for signs of welding; broken rods sometimes find their way out here.

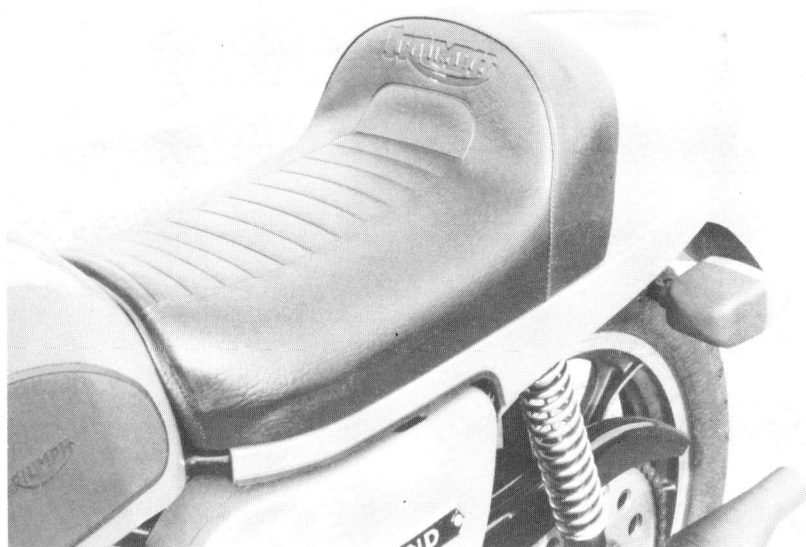

32

33

34

35

36

34.	Check the front down tube just above the engine mounting lug; has been known to crack – not very often.

35.	The sidestand lug sometimes bends: take a look at it.

36.	Slide the fork gaiters up and look at the stanchions; wear here can be clearly seen.

37.	Brake discs sometimes score badly: check them both. They can be skimmed if not too bad but replacement is expensive.

37

38

39

40

41

38. Trident assembly at Meriden before it moved to Birmingham.

39. In April 1974, Trident assembly was started at the BSA factory Small Heath, Birmingham. Strictly speaking it should be called the NVT factory. NVT had taken over

by that time and the Trident boasted a new type number, T160.

40. Another view of the T160 assembly line at Small Heath.

41. The engine assembly line at Small Heath, 1974. All three cylinder engines had been assembled at Small Heath right from the start.

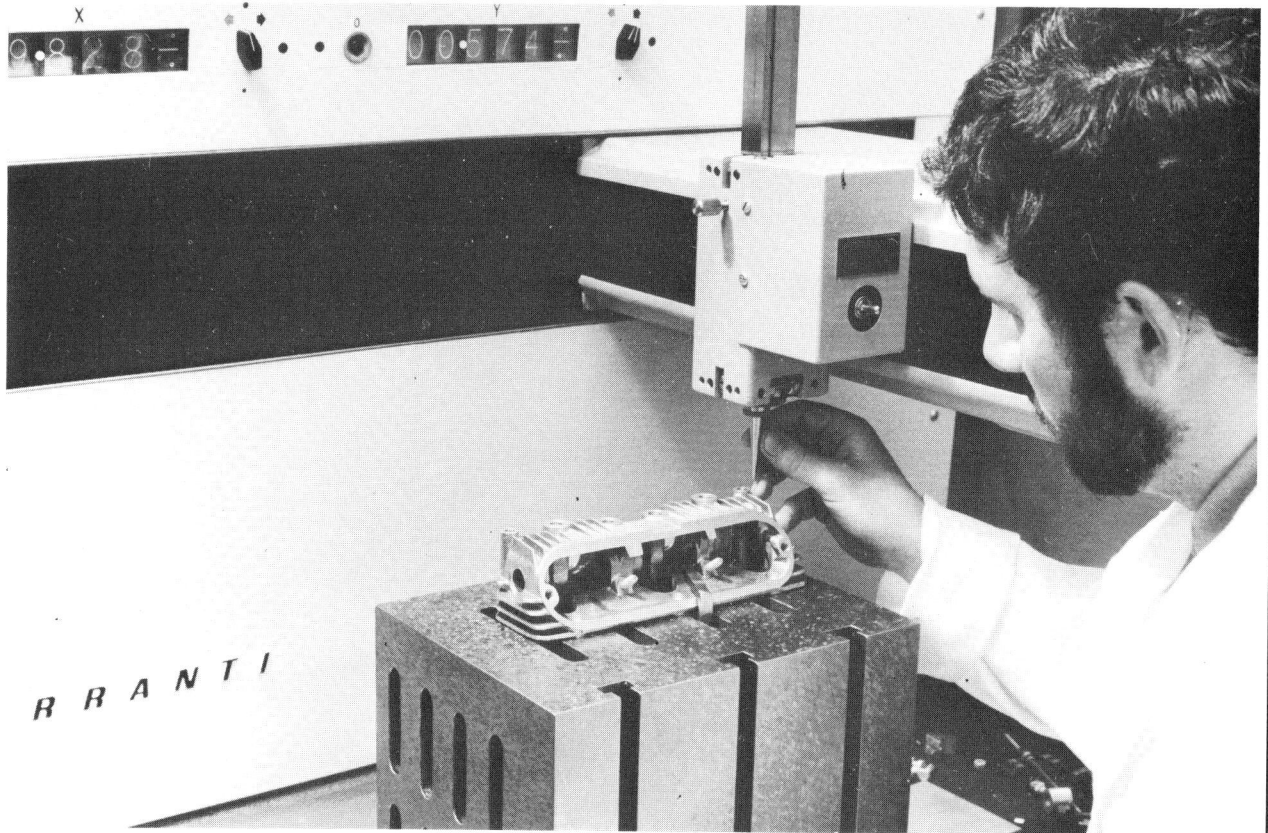

42. Ferranti inspection machine checking a T160 rocker box.

43. A prototype F750 Trident being put together in the Meriden race shop in 1971.

44

45

44 & 45. *1971 Daytona F750 obviously intended for Percy Tait.*

46, 47, 48.   Three unusual views of what is captioned as 'the ultimate 750' in the Trident racing line. Raced in '71 and '72.

46

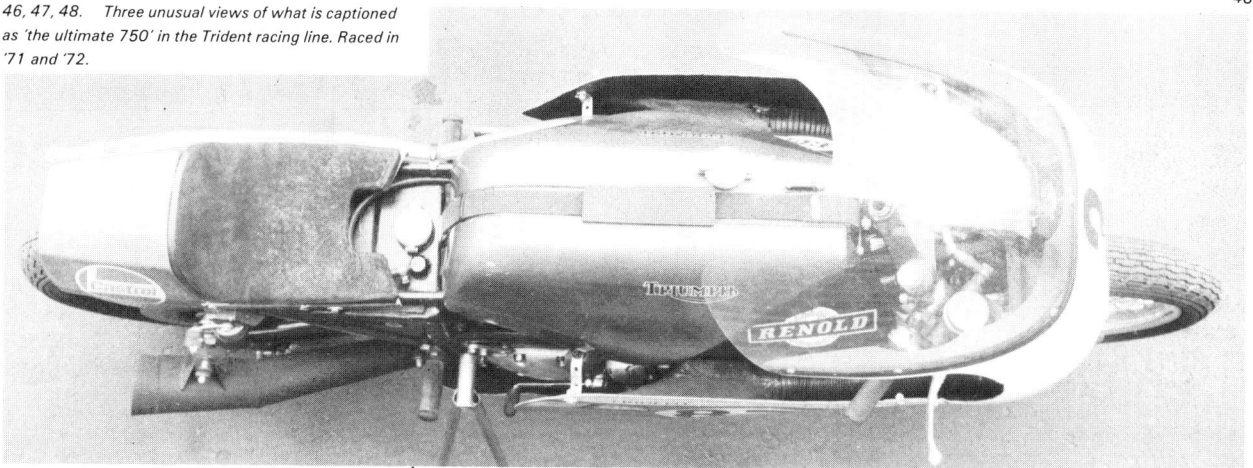

49

50

51

49. Ray Pickrell, winner of both the Production TT and the Formula 750 TT in the Isle of Man in 1972. He had many other victories to his credit.

50. Percy Tait on Slippery Sam. This celebrated model won the Production TT every year from 1971 to 1975. This shot shows Percy winning at Silverstone in 1973.

51. Tony Jefferies on his way to winning the Hutchinson 100 at Brands Hatch in 1971. John Cooper on a Rocket 3 was second, and claimed the fastest lap at 80.29 mph.

52. Mick Grant, winner of the 1974 Production TT on Slippery Sam, at 99.72mph.

53. A 1975 shot of Dave Croxford testing a 900cc engined Trident. Sadly, nothing came of it, both the Trident and the company reached the end of the line in this year.

54. Ray Pickrell and Slippery Sam on their way to winning the 1971 Production TT in the Isle of Man at 100.07 mph.

55

56

57

58

59

55.   A happy picture of John Cooper who, on his BSA triple, achieved undying fame by beating the reigning world champion Giacomo Agostini on his Grand Prix MV not once, but twice! The occasions were at the Race of the Year at Mallory Park in September 1971 and the Race of the South at Brands Hatch the following month.

56.   John Cooper in action on the BSA triple.

57.   'If you can't beat 'em join 'em' must be the title of this shot of Agostini having a gallop on a standard Trident at Mallory Park.

58.   Tridents were popular with 'privateers'. Here is Darryl Pendlebury of Coventry who finished 6th in the 1973 Production TT.

59.   Slippery Sam winner of five TTs, here seen with owner and tuner, Les Williams.

60.   A close-up of Ray Pickrell's Trident on which he
won the 1972 F750 TT at 105.68 mph.

60

61

61. The only BSA production racer produced at Meriden. It finished 3rd in the 1971 Production TT ridden by Bob Heath and won the 1971 Production Race at Silverstone in August 1971 in the hands of Ray Pickrell.

62. The triple ridden by John Cooper which defeater Agostini's grand prix MV twice. Seen on the front lawn at Meriden without its faiting.

62

63. In course of preparation at Meriden. This is the BSA triple which, ridden by American ace Dick Mann, won the 1971 Daytona race at 104.73 mph.

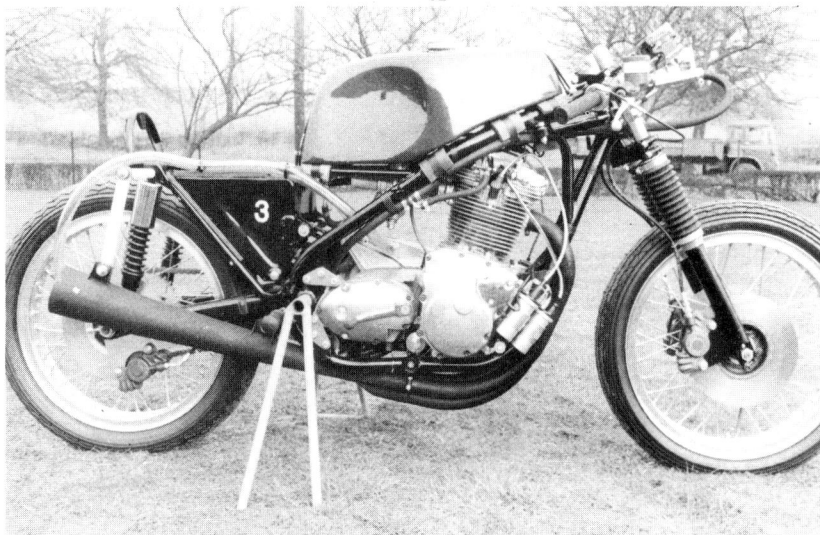

63

64

65

66

64. The Koelliker organisation in Milan were the Triumph distributors (they also sold Jaguars!) and they ran their own team of racing Tridents. The rider on this one is Gianfranco Bonero.

65. Not the most handsome Trident of all time, the Norman Hyde dragster! Norman is the holder of the World Sidecar Speed record at 161 mph with one of his Trident-engined monsters.

66. The Norman Hyde 850 cc barrel. The fins are fewer in number but thicker in section than the standard barrel. Also the top two fins are not recessed to take the pushrod tubes.

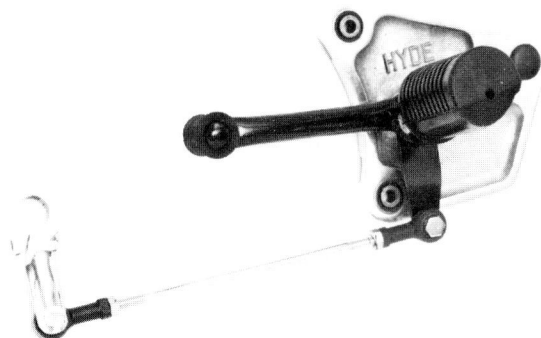
67

68

67 & 68. Robust rubber mounted footrest kits designed and supplied by Norman Hyde for Trident owners. The kit includes brake and gearchange pedals and all fixings.

69. BERT HOPWOOD F.I.Mech.E. held senior positions with Ariel, Triumph, Norton and BSA during his long career in the industry. Was largely responsible for bringing the Trident to the market plate where it would have arrived much earlier if things had gone as he planned and board room indecision and procrastination had not stood in the way.

70. DOUG HELE Chief Development Engineer Triumph Engineering Co Ltd who collaborated with Bert Hopwood right from the start in the design and development of the Trident. He will long be remembered for the way he masterminded its brilliant racing successes in the early seventies.

69

70

C1

C2

C1.   The standard Triumph twin leading shoe front brake was adopted for the Trident when it was announced in 1968.

C2.   The Trident fuel tank shape was unusual for Triumph, as was the colour – Aquamarine on the first models, it was changed a year later.

C3

C4

C3.   The Americans would not accept the square tank and for their market it quickly reverted to a more traditional shape as can be seen here. This is the 1971 US Trident.

C4.   The original tank was retained for most markets but it changed colour frequently. Here we have a 1974 T150.

C5

C6

C8

C7

C5.   The latest and last version of the Trident – the T160 where the tank shape has changed along with many other things.

C6.   There was a choice of two colours, red as in the previous picture, or yellow as here.

C7.   A close-up of the T160 power house. The tank shape is unusual for Triumph but quite pleasing.

C8.   What the pilot sees. Speedo, tacho and warning lights.

C9.

C10.

C9.   The most startling Trident of all – the X75 Hurricane with its way out styling. Many Jap bikes look like this today.

C10.   Another view of the Hurricane, probably the best angle to look at it.

C13

C11.   The Hurricane engine with its wider head fins than the standard Trident.

C12.   Hurricane forks, not quite to 'chopper' proportions but longer than the stock fork.

C13.   The original T150 silencers with the three small exit pipes were not popular – but this is going too far surely!! It could only happen on the X75.

C11

C12

C14

C15

C14, C15.   Trident into the eighties! The Les Williams 'Legend' a conversion from a customer's standard T160. Maybe the Trident would have looked like this today if it had still been in production.

C16

C17

C18

C16.   Trident into the eighties again! The Norman Hyde 1000cc 'Missile', a re-styled and re-engineered Trident, the 'Missile' is the product of Norman's years of experience as a development engineer at Meriden.

C17.   The 'Missile' front end with heavily braced stanchions, twin discs, and wire spoked wheels with alloy rim.

C18.   The 'Missile' back end with steeply canted suspension unit (or 'laid down shocks') and braced swinging fork leg.

C19

C20

C19.   A pleasing photograph from the Triumph
Publicity Department's file – just to remind us that
Trident ownership is not all about riding!

C20   Another publicity shot, this time outside the
ancient 'Queen and Castle' hotel in Kenilworth.